ASTRONOMY

YOU CAN NIBBLE

MEGAN BORGERT-SPANIOL

Consulting Editor, Diane Craig, MA/Reading Specialist

Super Sandcastle

An Imprint of Abdo Publishing
abdobooks.com

ABDOBOOKS.COM

Published by Abdo Publishing, a division of ABDO, PO Box 398166, Minneapolis, Minnesota 55439. Copyright © 2019 by Abdo Consulting Group, Inc. International copyrights reserved in all countries. No part of this book may be reproduced in any form without written permission from the publisher. Super SandCastle™ is a trademark and logo of Abdo Publishing.

Printed in the United States of America, North Mankato, Minnesota
102018
012019

THIS BOOK CONTAINS RECYCLED MATERIALS

Design: Emily O'Malley, Mighty Media, Inc.
Production: Mighty Media, Inc.
Editor: Liz Salzmann
Cover Photographs: Mighty Media, Inc.; Shutterstock
Interior Photographs: Mighty Media, Inc.; NASA; NASA Ames/JPL-Caltech/T Pyle; NASA/JPL-Caltech/Malin Space Science Systems; Shutterstock; Wikimedia Commons

The following manufacturers/names appearing in this book are trademarks:
Essential Everyday®, Nestle®, Old Home®, Oreo®, PAM®, Pillsbury Creamy Supreme®, Reynolds® Cut-Rite®, Roundy's®, Target®, Wilton® Candy Melts®, Wilton® Edible Accents™, Wilton® Pearl Dust™

Library of Congress Control Number: 2018948854

Publisher's Cataloging-in-Publication Data
Names: Borgert-Spaniol, Megan, author.
Title: Astronomy you can nibble / by Megan Borgert-Spaniol.
Description: Minneapolis, Minnesota : Abdo Publishing, 2019 | Series: Super simple science you can snack on
Identifiers: ISBN 9781532117220 (lib. bdg.) | ISBN 9781532170089 (ebook)
Subjects: LCSH: Astronomy--Juvenile literature. | Cooking--Juvenile literature. | Science--Experiments--Juvenile literature. | Gastronomy--Juvenile literature.
Classification: DDC 641.0--dc23

Super SandCastle™ books are created by a team of professional educators, reading specialists, and content developers around five essential components—phonemic awareness, phonics, vocabulary, text comprehension, and fluency—to assist young readers as they develop reading skills and strategies and increase their general knowledge. All books are written, reviewed, and leveled for guided reading and early reading intervention programs for use in shared, guided, and independent reading and writing activities to support a balanced approach to literacy instruction.

TO ADULT HELPERS

The projects in this book are fun and simple. There are just a few things to remember to keep kids safe. Some projects require the use of sharp or hot objects. Also, kids may be using messy ingredients. Make sure they protect their clothes and work surfaces. Review the projects before starting, and be ready to assist when necessary.

KEY SYMBOLS

Watch for these warning symbols in this book. Here is what they mean.

HOT!
You will be working with something hot. Get help!

SHARP!
You will be working with something sharp. Get help!

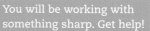

CONTENTS

WHAT IS ASTRONOMY?

Astronomy is a type of science. It is the study of objects in outer space. Outer space is the area outside Earth's atmosphere. Space objects include planets, stars, and moons.

Astronomers study space objects. Ancient astronomers observed those that could be seen with the naked eye. Later, telescopes and other tools were invented. These tools made it possible to see more of the universe.

EARTH HAS ONE MOON. SOME PLANETS HAVE MORE THAN ONE MOON. MARS HAS TWO. JUPITER HAS 79!

THE SUN IS ONE OF MANY BILLIONS OF STARS IN THE UNIVERSE.

GALILEO GALILEI

Many astronomers have helped advance the study of outer space. Important early astronomers included Nicolaus Copernicus, Galileo Galilei, and Edwin Hubble.

ASTRONOMY TODAY

Today, astronomers use **rovers**, spacecraft, and huge telescopes. These tools let astronomers study distant parts of our solar system. Astronomers can even study objects outside our solar system!

MARS ROVERS

The rover *Curiosity* landed on Mars in 2012. The rover is studying the planet's climate and **geology**. Another Mars rover launch is planned for 2020.

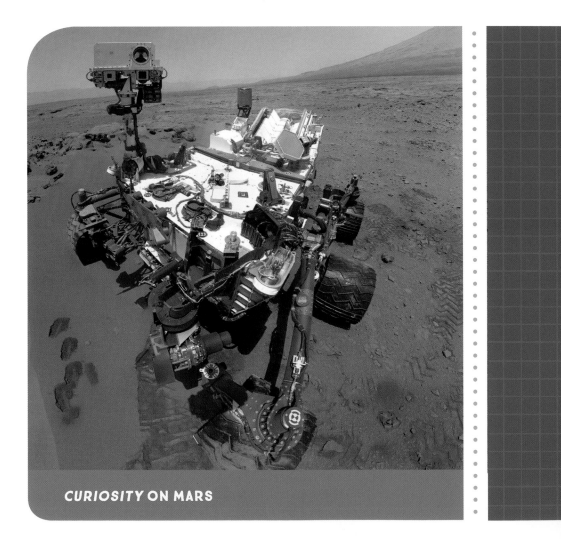

CURIOSITY **ON MARS**

A VOYAGER SPACECRAFT

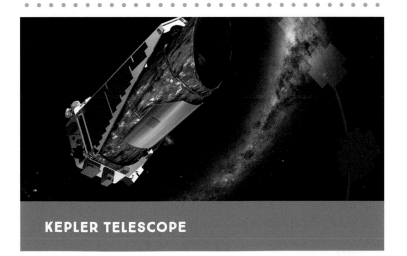

KEPLER TELESCOPE

VOYAGER PROBES

Twin **probes** *Voyager 1* and *Voyager 2* launched in 1977. They both explored Jupiter and Saturn. Then *Voyager 2* visited Uranus and Neptune while *Voyager 1* entered **interstellar space**. It was the first human-made object to go that far!

KEPLER SPACE TELESCOPE

The Kepler space telescope was launched in 2009. Its job was to find exoplanets. These are planets outside our solar system. By 2018, the telescope had found more than 2,000 exoplanets.

ASTRONOMY SNACKS

You can learn a lot about astronomy by making the fun snacks in this book!

GET READY

* Ask an adult for **permission** to use kitchen tools and ingredients.

* Read the snack's list of tools and ingredients. Make sure you have everything you need.

* Does a snack require ingredients you don't like? Get creative! Find other ingredients you enjoy instead.

SNACK CLEAN & SAFE

* Clean your work surface before you start.

* Wash your hands before you work with food.

* Keep your work area tidy. This makes it easier to find what you need.

* Ask an adult for help when handling sharp or hot objects.

CLEANING UP

* Don't waste unused ingredients! Store leftover ingredients to use later.

* Clean your work surface. Wash any dishes or tools you used.

* Wash your hands before you eat your snack!

INGREDIENTS & TOOLS

CANDY MELTS

CHOCOLATE CHIPS

CHOCOLATE FROSTING

CHOCOLATE SANDWICH COOKIES

CLEMENTINES

CRISPY RICE CEREAL

EDIBLE GLITTER DUST

GRAHAM CRACKERS

MINI MARSHMALLOWS

NON-STICK COOKING SPRAY

ROUND COOKIES

SMALL PRETZEL STICKS

STAR SPRINKLES

WHIPPED TOPPING

YOGURT

HERE ARE SOME OF THE INGREDIENTS AND TOOLS YOU WILL NEED TO MAKE THE SNACKS IN THIS BOOK.

ALUMINUM FOIL

BAKING SHEET

CONSTELLATION CHART

CUTTING BOARD

DINNER KNIFE

DRINKING GLASS

MEASURING CUPS

MICROWAVE-SAFE BOWL

PAINTBRUSH

PLASTIC ZIPPER BAGS

SCISSORS

SHARP KNIFE

SPATULA

WAX PAPER

WOODEN SKEWERS

TOOLS

SOLAR SYSTEM SNACK PLATE 🔪

INGREDIENTS

- assorted snacks (fruit, string cheese, mini marshmallows)
- yogurt
- clementine
- mini chocolate chips
- small pretzel stick

TOOLS

- sharp knife
- cutting board
- measuring cup
- plastic zipper bag
- scissors
- dark plate

Our solar system is made up of the sun and the objects that orbit it. These include planets, moons, and asteroids. You can make your own solar system out of bite-size snacks!

1. Cut any large snacks into bite-size pieces.

2. Pour 1 cup of yogurt into the plastic bag. Seal the bag.

3. Cut the tip off one of the bottom corners of the bag. This creates a small opening for **squeezing** the yogurt out of the bag.

4. Squeeze a dot of yogurt near the edge of the plate.

5. Squeeze an arc of yogurt around the dot.

6. Squeeze a larger arc of yogurt around the first arc.

7. Keep adding larger arcs of yogurt until there are nine arcs on the plate. This is the structure of your solar system.

Continued on the next page.

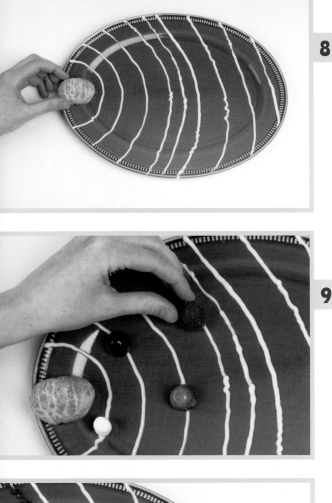

8. Peel the clementine. Break it in half. Place one half on top of the dot. This is the sun.

9. Place a bite-size snack on each of the first four arcs. These snacks represent the planets Mercury, Venus, Earth, and Mars.

10. Sprinkle mini chocolate chips along the fifth arc. The chips represent the asteroid belt.

11. Place snacks on the sixth and seventh arcs. These snacks represent Jupiter and Saturn. Add a piece of the pretzel stick on top of Saturn. This represents the planet's rings.

12. Place snacks on the two remaining arcs to represent Uranus and Neptune.

SCIENCE BITE

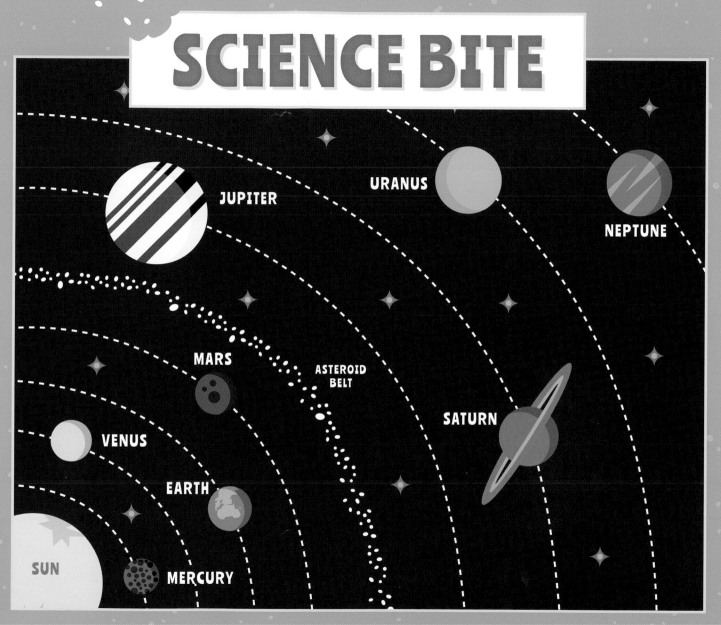

OUR SOLAR SYSTEM

MOON CAKE 🔥

INGREDIENTS

- non-stick cooking spray
- 4 tablespoons butter
- 16-ounce bag of mini marshmallows
- 4 cups crispy rice cereal
- 8 chocolate sandwich cookies
- 1½ cups whipped topping
- mini chocolate chips

TOOLS

- large microwave-safe bowl
- oven mitts
- spatula
- 2 medium bowls
- wax paper
- baking sheet
- large drinking glass
- aluminum foil
- plate for serving (optional)
- flag (optional)

Earth's moon is covered in craters. Craters form when large space objects hit the moon's surface. Make a crater-covered moon you can bite into!

1. Spray the large microwave-safe bowl and spatula with non-stick cooking spray.

2. Place the butter and 8 cups of marshmallows in the bowl.

3. Microwave the butter and marshmallows for 30 seconds. Stir.

4. Repeat step 3 until the marshmallows and butter are fully melted and combined.

5. Pour the crispy rice cereal into the bowl. Gently stir it into the marshmallow mixture.

6. Spray one of the medium bowls with non-stick cooking spray. Pour the cereal and marshmallow mixture into the medium bowl.

7. Use the spatula to pack the mixture into the bowl. Let the mixture cool.

Continued on the next page.

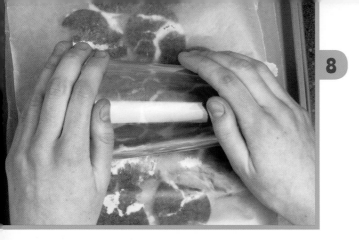

8

8. Place a sheet of wax paper on the baking sheet. Place the chocolate cookies on the wax paper. Cover them with another sheet of wax paper. Use the drinking glass to crush the cookies into **crumbs**.

9

9. Put the whipped topping in the other medium bowl. Mix the cookie crumbs into the whipped topping.

10. Line the baking sheet with foil. Set the bowl of cereal and marshmallow mixture upside down on the baking sheet. Lift the bowl to reveal the moon-shaped marshmallow treat.

10

11. Spread the whipped topping mixture evenly over the surface of the marshmallow moon.

12. Press marshmallows and chocolate chips onto the surface of the frosted treat. This will make the surface uneven, just like the moon's surface!

13. If you'd like, move your moon to a serving plate and top it with a flag!

S'MORE METEORITES 🔥

INGREDIENTS

- 6 ounces chocolate chips
- 4 full graham crackers
- 1½ cups mini marshmallows

TOOLS

- microwave-safe bowl
- oven mitts
- spatula
- baking sheet
- wax paper
- spoon

Meteorites are space rocks that hit Earth. They are often dark and crusty. This is because they burn as they enter Earth's atmosphere. Create some sweet meteorites to share with friends!

1. Pour the chocolate chips into the microwave-safe bowl.

2. Microwave the chips for 30 seconds. Stir.

3. Repeat step 2 until the chips are fully melted.

4. Break the graham crackers into bite-size pieces. Add them and the marshmallows to the bowl of chocolate.

5. Carefully stir until the chocolate coats everything.

6. Line the baking sheet with wax paper.

7. Place a spoonful of the mixture on the wax paper.

8. Repeat step 7 until the entire mixture has been divided into small clusters on the wax paper.

9. Place the baking sheet in the refrigerator for about 30 minutes. Then, bite into a meteorite!

EDIBLE CONSTELLATIONS

CASSIOPEIA

ORION

INGREDIENTS

- mini marshmallows
- small pretzel sticks

TOOL

- constellation chart

A pattern formed by stars is called a constellation. Find a constellation chart at the library or on the internet. Then build models of constellations out of marshmallows and pretzel sticks!

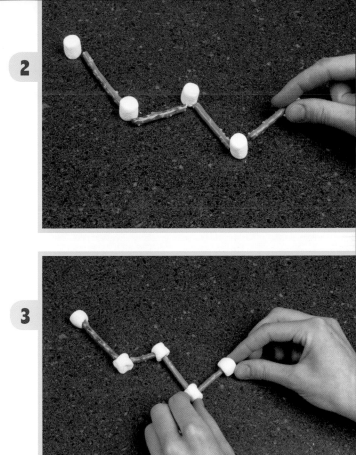

1. Choose a constellation from the constellation chart. Arrange marshmallows to represent the stars in the constellation.

2. Set pretzel sticks between the stars, matching the constellation's pattern. Break pretzel sticks into smaller pieces for stars that are closer together.

3. Make sure the constellation is arranged the way you want it. Push the pretzel sticks into the marshmallows to connect them.

4. Repeat steps 1 through 3 to create other **edible** constellations!

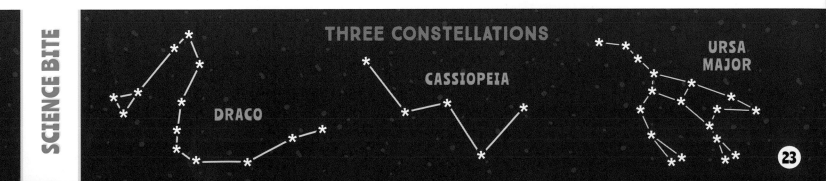

THREE CONSTELLATIONS

DRACO

CASSIOPEIA

URSA MAJOR

ICED ECLIPSE COOKIES

INGREDIENTS

- 5 round cookies
- chocolate frosting

TOOL

- dinner knife

The moon sometimes blocks sunlight from reaching Earth. This is called a solar eclipse. You can use cookies and frosting to create the phases of a total solar eclipse!

1. Lay the cookies in a row. Each cookie represents the sun.

2. Spread a **semicircle** of frosting onto the right edge of the first cookie. This is the moon starting to cover the sun.

3. Spread frosting over the second cookie. Leave a little bit of the left side unfrosted. This is the moon almost covering the sun.

4. Spread frosting over the center of the third cookie. Leave the edge of the cookie unfrosted. This is the moon centered over the sun. Only the sun's **corona** shows.

5. Spread frosting over the fourth cookie. Leave a little bit of the right side unfrosted. This is the moon starting to move to the other side of the sun.

6. Spread a semicircle of frosting onto the left edge of the fifth cookie. This is just before the moon moves away from the sun.

GALAXY BITES 🔥

INGREDIENTS

- 1 10-ounce bag black candy melts
- 1 cup purple candy melts
- 1 cup blue candy melts
- star sprinkles
- edible glitter dust

TOOLS

- baking sheet
- aluminum foil
- 3 microwave-safe bowls
- oven mitts
- spatulas
- wooden skewer
- clean paintbrush

A galaxy is a collection of gases, dust, and stars. Our solar system is in the Milky Way galaxy. The Milky Way looks like glowing bands of purple-blue light. Create this effect with candy melts!

1. Line the baking sheet with aluminum foil.

2. Put each color of candy in a separate microwave-safe bowl.

3. Microwave the black candy for 30 seconds. Stir.

4. Repeat step 3 until the black candy is fully melted.

5. Pour the candy onto the baking sheet. Spread it evenly.

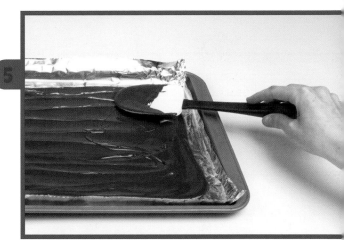

6. Repeat steps 3 and 4 to melt the purple and blue candy.

7. Pour the melted purple and blue candy over the black candy.

Continued on the next page.

8. Use the wooden skewer to **swirl** the colors together.

9. Sprinkle the candy with star sprinkles.

10. Place the baking sheet in the refrigerator for 20 minutes. This will harden the candy.

11. Brush **edible** glitter dust over the hardened candy.

12. Break your galaxy into pieces. Share the tasty treat with your friends!

SCIENCE BITE

THE MILKY WAY GALAXY AS SEEN FROM EARTH

CONCLUSION

Many space objects can be seen in the night sky. People have wondered at them for thousands of years. Astronomers study these objects. This helps them learn about the universe. Who knows what astronomers will discover next? Maybe they'll find life on other planets!

MAKING SNACKS IS JUST ONE WAY TO LEARN ABOUT ASTRONOMY. HOW WILL YOU CONTINUE YOUR ASTRONOMY ADVENTURE?

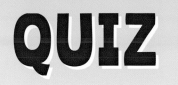

QUIZ

1. OUTER SPACE IS OUTSIDE EARTH'S ATMOSPHERE. TRUE OR FALSE?

2. WHAT ARE PLANETS OUTSIDE OUR SOLAR SYSTEM CALLED?

3. WHAT IS A CONSTELLATION?

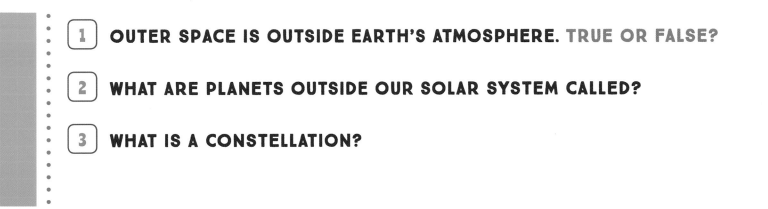

LEARN MORE ABOUT IT!

YOU CAN FIND OUT MORE ABOUT ASTRONOMY AT THE LIBRARY. OR YOU CAN ASK AN ADULT TO HELP YOU FIND INFORMATION ABOUT ASTRONOMY ON THE INTERNET!

ANSWERS: 1. TRUE 2. EXOPLANETS 3. A PATTERN OF STARS

GLOSSARY

corona – a bright circle of light around the sun or the moon. The sun's corona is especially visible during an eclipse.

crumb – a tiny piece of something, especially food.

edible – safe to eat.

geology – the structure and content of a space object.

interstellar space – the area outside Earth's solar system.

permission – when a person in charge says it's okay to do something.

probe – a spacecraft that attempts to gather information.

rover – a vehicle used for exploring the surface of space objects.

semicircle – half of a circle.

squeeze – to press or grip something tightly.

swirl – to whirl or to move smoothly in circles.